THIS IS ME!

SILLY RHYMES AND SERIOUS THOUGHTS

Edited By Lynsey Evans

First published in Great Britain in 2024 by:

YoungWriters®
Est. 1991

Young Writers
Remus House
Coltsfoot Drive
Peterborough
PE2 9BF
Telephone: 01733 890066
Website: www.youngwriters.co.uk

Printed and bound in the UK by BookPrintingUK
Website: www.bookprintinguk.com
YB0MA0047A

FOREWORD

For Young Writers' latest competition This Is Me,
we asked primary school pupils to look inside
themselves, to think about what makes them unique,
and then write a poem about it! They rose to the
challenge magnificently and the result is this fantastic
collection of poems in a variety of poetic styles.

Here at Young Writers our aim is to encourage creativity
in children and to inspire a love of the written word, so
it's great to get such an amazing response, with some
absolutely fantastic poems. It's important for children to
focus on and celebrate themselves and this competition
allowed them to write freely and honestly, celebrating
what makes them great, expressing their hopes and
fears, or simply writing about their favourite things.
This Is Me gave them the power of words. The result
is a collection of inspirational and moving poems that
also showcase their creativity and writing ability.

I'd like to congratulate all the young poets
in this anthology, I hope this inspires them
to continue with their creative writing.

CONTENTS

| Leo Bower (8) | 48 |

Camphill Primary School, Ballymena

| Aria Mcilrath (9) | 49 |
| Leo Balmer (10) | 50 |

Catrine Primary School, Catrine

Hannah Mackenzie (10)	51
Eilidh Childs (9)	52
Lucy Gillies (10)	53
Caleb Davidson (10)	54
Jalyn Seaton (9)	55
Olly McDowall (10)	56

Chapelside Primary School, Airdrie

Carly Love (8)	57
Macie Karen Renwick (8)	58
Jace Chapman (8)	59

Christ The King Catholic Primary School, Stockton-On-Tees

Myla-Rae Jobson (9)	60
Nancy Cheesebrough (9)	61
Amy Rossel (9)	62
Roman West (9)	63
Reuben Edmonds (9)	64
Leo Simm (9)	65

Copmanthorpe Primary School, Copmanthorpe

| Poppy Guest (9) | 66 |
| Evie Appleton (10) | 67 |

Dovedale Primary School, Long Eaton

| Henry Shaw (10) | 68 |
| Oscar Bailey (9) | 69 |

Sahil Avasthy (9)	70
Noah Mitchell (9)	71
Harrison Sage (10)	72
Layla Rose Day (9)	73
Lilly Dudley (10)	74
Andrei Florescu (10)	75
Bethan James (9)	76
Luca Needham (9)	77
Blake Hamblett (9)	78
Jayden Tavernor (9)	79

Downsview Primary School, Upper Norwood

Amelia Allen (11)	80
Rose Stewart (9)	81
Iman	82
Lili Owen (10)	84
Megan	85
Raabia	86
Leonardo Kim Sing (6)	87

Fair Isle Primary School, Kirkcaldy

| Kole Dolan (9) | 88 |

Heamoor Community Primary School, Heamoor

| George Chisnall (9) | 89 |

Heath Lane Academy, Earl Shilton

| Jasmine Elverstone (13) | 90 |

Heathrow Primary School, Sipson

Taqweem Hassan (10)	91
Emaan Bilal (7)	92
Daksh Devasi (7)	93
Harriet Coughlan (9)	94
Phoebe Whitehead-Collins (10)	95
Dinah Umair (7)	96
Banee Dhutti (9)	97

Divraj Sidhu (9)   98

High Crags Primary Leadership Academy, Shipley

Nevaeh Renee Lawrence (10)   99
Arya Field (10)   100

Horrington Primary School, West Horrington

Eli Webb (8)   101

Hungerford Primary School, Hungerford

Ryley-Mclaren Howard (9)   102
Casey Scarlett (9)   103

Kirkshaws Primary School, Coatbridge

Kade Wilson (8)   104
Maddison McGraw (8)   105
Reuben Kennedy (9)   106

Lea St Mary's Catholic Primary School, Preston

Georgia Purkis (10)   107
Dante Lewis (10)   108

Locharbriggs Primary School, Locharbriggs

Emmy Macdonald (9)   109
Cory Fraser (9)   110
Jamie Saunders (9)   111

Loretto RC Primary School, Musselburgh

Murren Manning (11)   112
Flavio Ccarlo (11)   113

Merriott Primary School, Merriott

Reggie Martin (9)   114

Newberries Primary School, Radlett

Quinn Brander-Stark (8)   115
Jaejah Sullivan (8)   116

North Petherton Community Primary School, North Petherton

Oscar Morrison (8)   117
Holly Davis (7)   118
Harry Lloyd (7)   119
Edith Court (7)   120
Elliott Jones (7)   121

Peel Primary School, Eliburn East

Suraya Kamara (9)   122

Pencoed Primary School, Pencoed

Isabella Patrick (11)   123
Clara Curtis (9)   124
Zara Jones (9)   126
Sophia Davies (10)   128
Isabella Evans (10)   129
Ruby Hancock (9)   130
Bella Gill (10)   132
Oliver Jones (10)   134
Poppy Burgess (9)   135
Seren-Jade Gilboy (10)   136
Mia-Bella Porter (9)   137
Ethan Ford (9)   138
Will Powell (10)   139
Freya Beckinsale (10)   140
Lucas Austin (10)   141
Sophie Oliver (9)   142
Harrison Coburn (10)   143
Brandon Brandon (10)   144
Tillie Lovell (10)   145

Petersfield CE (A) Primary School, Orwell

Ronnie Van der Merwe (9)	146
Leo Alexander (10)	147
Beatrice McKenzie (10)	148

Prenton Primary School, Prenton

Daisy Hardy (10)	149
Olivia Morrell (10)	150
Samuel Dunning (8)	151
Ben Dunning (9)	152

Rathfern Primary School, London

Kamal Owolabi (8)	153

Rillington Community Primary School, Rillington

Santino Abbey (7)	154

Rothley CE Primary Academy, Rothley

Johnny Morgun (7)	155
Oliver Reid	156

Sacred Heart Catholic Primary School, Middlesbrough

Joan Ejakpovi (9)	157
Norah Sibi (7)	158

Shavington Primary School, Shavington

Aaliyah Jones (9)	160
Archie Clark-Owen (7)	161
Poppy Carney (9)	162
Arlia Fayers (9)	163
Savannah Pourawal (7)	164
Eliza Randle (8)	165
Ivy Banks (8)	166
Lillia Phillips (8)	167

William Jasinski (9)	168
Kimmy Li (9)	169
Poppy Wood (7)	170
Sasha Pourawal (10)	171
Isabella Thompson-Edge (7)	172
Lucas Li (7)	173
Brody Xennon Steele (8)	174

Simonside Community Primary School, Newcastle Upon Tyne

Limar Ahmad (9)	175
Lilly Rae (10)	176

Spalding St Paul's Primary School, Spalding

Natalia Tanska (9)	177
Elsie Purvis (7)	178
Toby Waltham (8)	179

St Aidan's Primary School, Wishaw

Nicole Szczepanski (10)	180

St Bernard's Catholic Primary School, Birmingham

Simra Khan (7)	181
Anaya Fatima (8)	182
Ruqaya Hussain (7)	183
Ilayda Kaplan (9)	184
Anya Noor Ali (8)	185
Ibrahim Bahakam (7)	186
Ayesha Mohmand (8)	187
Aleef Aklaq (7)	188
Zayan Ali	189
Muhammad Aayan (7)	190

St David's Prep School, Purley

Myan Patel (7)	191
Elena Wan (8)	192

St Helen's Primary School, Bishopbriggs

Chinecherem Okafor (11)	193
Lila Whitelaw (8)	194
Millie Corr (10)	195
Oscar Forde (11)	196
Aailah Choudry (8)	197
Cian Owens (11)	198
Bradley McAllister (11)	199
Mohammed Rehaan Choudry (11)	200
Finlay Lundie (11)	201
Alyssa Graham (11)	202
Christopher McKechnie (10)	203
Amelia Hampsey (11)	204
Anthony Cosgrove (11)	205

St Joseph & St Teresa's Catholic Primary School, Woodlands

Kashana Mapemba (9)	206
Jacob Hodgson (10)	208
Sapphire-Rose Spencer (9)	210
Annalee Biggings (9)	211
Jethro Scott (8)	212
Summer Nelson (10)	213
Ellie Wrafter-Saxton (8)	214
Skyla Wilkinson (8)	216
Maxim Pavlovskij (8)	217
Sapphire Wright (10)	218
Libby Headrigi (10)	219
Flynn O'Connell (7)	220

St Margaret's CE Primary School, Horsforth

Kamran Buck (9)	221
Jenson Stewart (9)	222

St Mary's CE Primary School, Hinckley

Adrijus Zygmantas (9)	223
Amelia Davies (9)	224
Isaac Linton (10)	226

Lucia Harrison (11)	227
Morgan Stevens (11)	228
Ethan Oppong (9)	229
Kamil Czarnecki (11)	230
Harry Proctor (11)	231

St Mary's Church Of England (Voluntary Aided) Primary School, Swanley

Isaac Waterman (10)	232

St Patrick's Primary School, Moneymore

Andis (Toby) Kalnins (11)	233

St Robert Southwell Catholic Primary School, Horsham

Sidney Jubb (9)	234
Santiago Fernandes (9)	235
Theo Strutt (9)	236
Ronnie Digweed Ball (10)	237

St Thomas CE Primary School, Werneth

Labaika Mahmood (9)	238

Welton Primary School, Brough

Saleh Altaf (9)	239

Whirley Primary School, Macclesfield

Annabel Jones (10)	240
Bella Hill (10)	241

Windlesham School & Nursery, Brighton

Matilda King (11)	242

Woodlawn Primary School, Carrickfergus

Andrew Sloss-Hartley (8)	243
Riley O'Lynn (8)	244
Freddie Anderson (9)	245
Kobi Wylie (9)	246
Zac Berry (8)	247
Ellie Whiteside (8)	248
Noah Hollis (8)	249

THE POEMS

Evacuees

I got on the train, sadly saying goodbye to Mother
It was a sad journey on the way

But when we got there, I was looked after with care
There was another child called Arthur
He was an evacuee, too

One day, I noticed a monster in the garden
It had huge horns, hooves and a shining ring on the nose

I ran in to tell Jade, my guardian, about this beast
But he said, "It's just a cow, it gives you milk"

The next day I was sent away back to my home
I was happy
I squeezed Mother in a really big hug
It was finally over
I was home.

Henry Wills (9)
Aldwickbury School, Harpenden

Halloween

H alloween is the best
A t Halloween, we get sweets
L ovely costumes
L ovely scary costumes
O h! I'm always so scared
W e go out trick-or-treating
E veryone together
E veryone in our street
N ow we eat all our sweets.

Keiva Martin (8)
Balmuildy Primary School, Bishopbriggs

Badminton

B adminton is my main sport with
A dvantages such as agility which
D esign a
M ild
I ntellect
N ot
T ennis
O h
N o.

Henry Martin (10)
Benedict House Preparatory School, Sidcup

This Is Me!

If my name was a fruit it would be
Mango reflecting the glowing sunlight.
If my name was a colour my name would be
Pink like a tree blossoming in the summer.
If my name was a sport it would be
Football winning the Champions League
If my name was a drink my name would be
Oasis on a hot summer day
If my name was a sound my name would be
Waves crashing against the rocks
If my name was a football team I would be
Leeds United scoring whenever I can
If my name was a football player my name would be
Ella Toone bringing it home
If my name was an emotion my name would be
Joy! Like a toddler eating McDonald's.
This is me!

Heidi Thorpe (10)
Brockholes Wood Primary School, Preston

If My Name Was

If my name was a person, it would be Hazza.

If my name was a YouTuber, it would be me.

If my name was a country, it would be England because of the nature and animals.

If my name was a F1 driver it would be Max Verstappen because he flies around the Japanese Grand Prix track on a rainy day.

If my name was a food, it would be sushi.

Harry Rigby (10)
Brockholes Wood Primary School, Preston

Deep, Dark Halloween

Scary orange pumpkins
Creepy-crawly spiders
White bony skeletons
Invisible creaky ghosts
Deep, dark costumes
Flickering dark light
Mysterious scary trick-or-treating
Dangling spooky decorations

This is Halloween!

Vincent Kay (9)
Brockholes Wood Primary School, Preston

This Is Me

Kicking is crucial, so are you
Now let's test your knowledge too,
Passing, tackling, shooting, scoring,
Since he can score, then so can you,
Cardiff vs Rotherham 2-0,
Don't worry, you still did good,
Well rated player,
Doesn't always win but doesn't always lose.

Who am I?

Channel Karanja (9)

Brookfield Junior Academy, Swinton

Roblox

R oblox is really fun
O nly if my brother plays
B rookhaven is the best game ever
L ook at Brookhaven, it's the best
O h I just love Brookhaven
X says my brother.

Emma Turton (6)

Brookfield Junior Academy, Swinton

All About Me

L uca loves Lego and Roblox
U nicorns are not my type
C an't play football
A fan of Harvey's jokes.

Luca-Jae McCloud (7)

Brookfield Junior Academy, Swinton

My Name

P retty

O ranges are sweet

P ink

P oppy has a little sister

Y esterday I saw my friend Maisy.

Poppy McKee (5)

Brookfield Junior Academy, Swinton

My Name

J ogging is fun
A cat purrs
C ake I like is chocolate
O ranges are sweet
B irds.

Jacob Shaw (6)

Brookfield Junior Academy, Swinton

This Is Me!

K ites are fun
Y ou are funner
L ove friends and family
A s well as teachers.

Kyla Shaw (8)
Brookfield Junior Academy, Swinton

This Is Me!

K ites are fun
Y ou are funner
L ove friends and family
A s well as teachers.

Kyla Shaw (8)
Brookfield Junior Academy, Swinton

12

I Am Me

I am positive

I am positive when I see my family and friends,
I am like a jumping kangaroo jumping up and down,
I am like a silly dog wagging its tail,
I am me.

I am sad

I am sad when I feel like the only fish in the sea,
I am like melting chocolate,
I am me.

I am happy

I am like one million smiling faces mixing together,
I am like a waterfall and the water going down is about to burst,
I am me.

Lily Taylor
Cadbury Heath Primary School, Warmley

I Can Only Be Me

I am excited

I am excited when I sing and dance,
I am excited like a fantasy fairy when I get to do something fun that I like,
I am excited like a puppy when I get to go to my favourite place,
I am excited when Jaiden has done brilliant writing and spelling,
I am me.

I am loving

I am loving when I feel very warm and cosy,
I am loving like a Valentine's teddy bear,
I am loving like a happy cute baby,
I am loving when I feel cuddly and happy,
I am me.

I am confident

I am confident when I play games,
I am confident when I show someone something I'm proud of,

I am as confident as a famous singer,
I am confident when I read to someone out loud,
I am me
And no one can stop me from being myself.

Alula Edmonds (10)

Cadbury Heath Primary School, Warmley

I Am Me

Loved

I am loved,
I love it when it's Christmas,
I like doing gymnastics,
I love being me,
I am me.

Being me

I am brave,
I am as powerful as a magician,
I like Halloween when we dress up,
I am myself and nobody can stop that,
I am me.

Being happy

I am happy,
I am as happy as a bunny eating carrots,
I am creative,
I am confident,
I am me.

Grateful

I am playful,
I will do anything I put my mind to,
I am as fast as a cheetah,
I can't stop being me,
I am grateful, I am myself,
I am me.

Sienna May Smith (10)

Cadbury Heath Primary School, Warmley

This Is Me!

I am excited

I am excited when it's Christmas,
I am as excited as a bunny getting carrots,
I am me.

I am loved

I am loved when I do good things,
I am as loved as a teddy bear,
I am me.

I am happy

I am happy when I get noodles,
I am as happy as a guinea pig getting spinach,
I am me.

I am sad

I am sad when nobody wants to play with me,
I am as sad as a crying baby,
I am me.

I am angry

I am angry when I get teased,
I am as angry as a lion,
I am me.

Ruby Smith (10)
Cadbury Heath Primary School, Warmley

I Am Me

I am happy playing football,
I'm like a tornado tearing between the opposition.
When I play football
I am me.

I'm anxious,
I feel anxious when I play football in front of my
parents,
I am me.

I am excited to see Harry and Fletcher,
I like a pig rolling in the mud,
I am me.

Rupert Conroy (9)
Cadbury Heath Primary School, Warmley

This Is Me

I am hungry when I get home from school,
I am hungry when I am on my iPad,
I am like a hungry lion waiting for his food.

I am happy when it is Tuesday,
I am happy when I get my iPad,
I am as happy as a puppy.

I am loved at home,
I am loved at school,
I am loved and liked.

Poppy Robertson (9)
Cadbury Heath Primary School, Warmley

All About Me

My name is Ruby, my surname is Dacey.
I have a pet dog, she is an XL Bully.
My favourite food is a takeaway.
I have brown eyes and blonde and brown hair.
I love going swimming with the school.
I am sporty and chatty.
I take my dog out to her favourite places which are the beach and pet shop
And I always save my money for my dog and I let her pick what she wants.
My best friends are Lexi, Hattie, Sienna, Elena, my mum, dad and my family.
I go to my favourite places with Lexi and the people in my class.
My birthday is February 11th.

Ruby Dacey (9)

Caister Junior School, Caister-On-Sea

Guess My Dog's Breed

I play with her every day.

She needs to go for a walk twice a day.

She moults like crazy.

My mum hoovers every day 'cause the house is full of fluff.

She has a lot of energy.

She loves treats.

She has huge paws, like the size of my hand.

She eats treats in about 10 seconds.

She always takes my teddies or plays with her own.

She's so fluffy and stupid

But I love her.

Cassidy Devine (10)
Caister Junior School, Caister-On-Sea

My Recipe Poem

First, gather caring and kindness.
Stir in football and AstroTurf.
Season with watching and playing football.
Add a pinch of knowing you are not the captain.
Pour in a dog's playfulness
And a bowl of energy in the morning.
Blend Christmas and my birthday
Then warm gently by lying in my bed
While I talk to my friends and play FIFA.

Grayson George (9)

Caister Junior School, Caister-On-Sea

McDonald's Is My Home

McDonald's is my home.

I eat all the nuggets alone.

A Big Mac will always do

But if they get it wrong I will sue.

Millions of customers but I am number one.

No one can stop me from pushing to the front.

I like McDonald's because it always has the snacks

But you can only get McDonald's if you have the racks.

Jenson Savage (10)

Caister Junior School, Caister-On-Sea

Loo Loo Lexi

I'm sweet but I'm sour
I'm about to devour
Depends on the hour
I'm about to get in the shower
Yes, woo!

I just got out of the shower
It was a good hour
Now it's time to watch
A very funny vine.

I'm very funny
But a bit of a dummy
This is me!

Lexi Hill (10)
Caister Junior School, Caister-On-Sea

All About Me

First, gather personality and bravery.
Stir in football and my dog and TV.
Season with games of football.
Add a pinch of adventure.
Pour in a bit of fun walks
And a lovely bit of pizza.
Blend in energy every lovely morning.
Then warm gently by loving cold Christmas.

Bella Burman (9)
Caister Junior School, Caister-On-Sea

All About Me

I'm bendy like a ruler.

Taller than a drooler.

Smaller than a hooter.

I'm better at climbing than I am at rhyming.

Can't you see I'm really trying to finish my rhyming

As I'm lying in bed while trying to sort out my timing.

Rose Crowe (10)

Caister Junior School, Caister-On-Sea

This Is Me

I am a...

Dog lover
Halloween scarer
Money maker
Chocolate eater
Popcorn taster
Blue lover
Maths learner
Fast runner
Easter egg finder
Singer/dancer
Toy sharer
Good helper

This is me.

Heath Bullimore (7)
Caister Junior School, Caister-On-Sea

This Is Me

T he kid loves his family
H aving my life is nice
I watch movies with my family
S uper kid

I 'm kind
S uper kind

M ega gamer
E ven New Year's Eve is great.

Riley-Kai Bridge (10)
Caister Junior School, Caister-On-Sea

Me

Lego of all shapes and colours
I have a cute little fur ball
I like scary, slimy snakes in all different colours
Red for angry
Blue for sadness
Yellow for happiness
I like making gingerbread men
I like eating them too.

Roman Buillmore (9)

Caister Junior School, Caister-On-Sea

This Is Me

I am a...
Pokémon player
Chocolate eater
Taekwondo kicker
Basketball player
Cookie eater
Game player
Ice cream eater
Animal lover
Tablet gamer
Artist
This is me!

Joseph Allen (7)
Caister Junior School, Caister-On-Sea

My Personality

I am a...
Book reader
Footballer
Chocolate eater
Cricketer
Archer
Gamer
Game maker
Goalkeeper
Striker
Defender
Winger
Midfielder

This is me.

Archer Hacon (9)
Caister Junior School, Caister-On-Sea

This Is Me

I am a...
Dancing ballerina
Ice cream eater
Rainbow cake eater
Cake eater
Apple eater
Gymnastics lover
Family hugger
Nature lover
This is me.

Melanie Karpowicz (7)

Caister Junior School, Caister-On-Sea

Me

To be me you will need...
A lot of happiness
Some arts and crafts
And a lot of books
And a pinch of mean
And a lot of kindness
And that is me.

Tyra Clegg (9)
Caister Junior School, Caister-On-Sea

Me

I am a...
Summer lover
Music listener
Book reader
McDonald's eater
Muffin lover
Dog lover
Hot chocolate drinker
Game player.

Poppy Barron (10)

Caister Junior School, Caister-On-Sea

It Is All About Me

I am good at football
I'm confident, that's what I like about me.
I am bendy like a ruler.
What makes me happy is my family and my animals.

Amelia Johnson (10)

Caister Junior School, Caister-On-Sea

All About Me

I am a...
Art drawer.
Soup slurper.
Happy learner.
Film watcher.
Turkey girl.
Water drinker.
That is me!

Zeynab Gilgil (7)
Caister Junior School, Caister-On-Sea

This Is Me

I am a...

Harry Potter lover
English lover
Dog lover
Hard worker
History lover

This is me.

Teddy Barron (7)
Caister Junior School, Caister-On-Sea

This Is Me

Puppy lover
Stitch lover
Book reader
Christmas decorator
TV watcher
Drawing lover

This is me.

Jessica Allright (7)
Caister Junior School, Caister-On-Sea

This Is Me

I am a...

Chocolate eater
Christmas enthusiast
YouTube watcher
Birthday lover

This is me.

Harry Parker (7)
Caister Junior School, Caister-On-Sea

All About Me

I am a...
Good swimmer.
Fast eater.
Basketball player.
Gaming player.
Yo-yo eater.
This is me.

Jack Bolton (7)
Caister Junior School, Caister-On-Sea

This Is Me

I like playing football
And I like playing Fortnite.
I like to go to the park.
I like it when school is over.

Jaken Royden (9)
Caister Junior School, Caister-On-Sea

This Is Me

I am a...

Dog lover
Candyfloss eater
Good mathematician
Oasis drinker

This is me.

William (7)
Caister Junior School, Caister-On-Sea

This Is Me!

T hird top goal scorer in football.

H opeful all the time.

I have three brothers, but they are really, really mean.

S uper keeper in goal, but I want to go in the right wing.

I have a dog called Bella, and she is so cute, and she is a chihuahua.

S weeping is the best chore.

M aking brownies for my team.

E xciting keeper.

Harrison Payne (8)

Calmore Junior School, Calmore

This Is Me

T op at art, I think.

H arry Potter fan.

I always play with Daisy.

S uper smart.

I ntelligent.

S uper eat.

M y family means the most to me.

E lisiya is my name.

Elisiya Sutton (8)

Calmore Junior School, Calmore

I'm A...

I'm a lightning bolt
I'm a goal-scorer
I'm a chef
I am a goalie
I am a cake baker
I have brown marbles for eyes
I'm probably faster than you
I have fish, dogs and hamsters.

Logan Hicks (8)
Calmore Junior School, Calmore

This Is Me!

My name is Leo!
I am an artist,
An alien creator,
A character creator,
A tennis creator,
A creator is who I am!

Leo Bower (8)
Calmore Junior School, Calmore

My Kennings - About Me

Amazing footballer
Chelsea supporter
Cat hater
Great artist
Swimming lover
Great sister
Holiday goer
Goalkeeper lover
Outdoors lover
Expert dancer
Phone addict
Music lover
Home lover
Hungry eater.

Aria Mcilrath (9)
Camphill Primary School, Ballymena

My Kennings

Football expert
BMX rider
Pro gamer
MF fighter
Manchester fan
Science lover.

Leo Balmer (10)

Camphill Primary School, Ballymena

Hannah's Life

H air like a grizzly bear.

A m very talkative and I am as kind as a nurse.

N ike is my favourite brand.

N ike 270s are my favourite trainers.

A tub of Ben & Jerry's ice cream is the best.

H annah is my name.

S prite is a drink I like and I am as in love with chocolate as Willy Wonka.

L ife is fun.

I love my dogs and friends.

F raser is my dad.

E llie is my best friend.

Hannah Mackenzie (10)

Catrine Primary School, Catrine

Eilidh's Life

J oma Jewellery is the best.

E nergetic is the way to describe me.

W onderful at dance.

E llie, Hannah, Koko and Lucy are my BFFs.

L ove my dog and love Nike.

L ovely and kind.

E llie Goulding and Calvin Harris have good music.

'R' is in 'trampoline' and I have one.

Y ummy chocolate is very good.

Eilidh Childs (9)
Catrine Primary School, Catrine

Lucy's Life

L oving and caring,
U nicorns are amazing,
C risps are the best,
Y MCA is fun,
S miling is my hobby.

L exi is my best friend,
I love Nike Techs,
F rom Catrine,
E llie is brilliant.

Lucy Gillies (10)

Catrine Primary School, Catrine

My Christmas

C hristmas carolling

H oly Spirit

R unning in the snow

I s it snowing?

S o much joy!

T urkey

M erry Christmas

A merry man

S o many presents to give out.

Caleb Davidson (10)

Catrine Primary School, Catrine

Jalyn Says Hey

I am as brave as a bear
A denim dress I like to wear
I like dogs
I am as sporty as a football player
My best pals are Millie and Harper
I like swimming because it's winning
I like ham
I am good at gymnastics.

Jalyn Seaton (9)
Catrine Primary School, Catrine

Juicy As An Orange

I am as kind as a fly,
I love dogs,
I love fruit, especially oranges,
I love chicken nuggets,
I love my PlayStation 5,
I love my house.

Olly McDowall (10)
Catrine Primary School, Catrine

Poetry

H urry up

A nd PE kit

N oble Celts

D oing cartwheels

S plits

T umble

A shoulder stand

N o heroics

D o be safe!

Carly Love (8)

Chapelside Primary School, Airdrie

Family

F un
A larming
M ental
I nterrupting
L ots of brains
Y oung.

Macie Karen Renwick (8)
Chapelside Primary School, Airdrie

Cats

C lawing

A toy of yours

T rees are what they climb

S o fluffy!

Jace Chapman (8)

Chapelside Primary School, Airdrie

This Is Me!

T his is Myla speaking!

H ope you're ready for my poem.

I 'm very funny, sometimes I get too funny.

S martly, I'm brainy like my favourite animal, a mangy monkey.

I love everyone, just like I love you!

S ometimes I act like a monkey.

M yla is my name.

E lephants are my second favourite animal!

Myla-Rae Jobson (9)

Christ The King Catholic Primary School, Stockton-On-Tees

All About Me!

T reasured by my family

H ave many awesome qualities.

I love my dog, Rocky.

S cared of what's in the dark

I really love my rabbit

S atisfied by the steak from the Griffin

M e and my friends like to play police interceptors

E ggs are nice, especially with soldiers.

Nancy Cheesebrough (9)

Christ The King Catholic Primary School, Stockton-On-Tees

My Recipe

To make me, you need:
A book-filled room
A personality of a dog
Lots of Stitch stuff
My BFFs Oyin, Harriet and Mia
Arty things
A jar full of kindness
Two spoonfuls of happiness
Every subject but not maths!

This is my recipe!
Bye!

Amy Rossel (9)
Christ The King Catholic Primary School, Stockton-On-Tees

Wonder World

I like swimming instead of singing
I like sizzling sausages on the see-saw
I have a snake, trust me it is not great.
I have a snake and I am not fake
I like cooking things, but most end up in the bins
I can see this is me.

Roman West (9)
Christ The King Catholic Primary School, Stockton-On-Tees

The Boy's Poem Of The Year

Hi, I'm Reuben
I'm as slick as a snake
I'm as big as a bear
I'm not a fake
I'm out with the boys
Every day,
Look at me
Look at me
This is me!

Reuben Edmonds (9)

Christ The King Catholic Primary School, Stockton-On-Tees

Can You Make Me?

Lots of nice clothes
A massive bedroom
Lots of fun toys
A gaming room
20 pounds of pizza
200 kilos of fun and mischief.

Leo Simm (9)

Christ The King Catholic Primary School, Stockton-On-Tees

This Is Me

My name is Poppy,
I like to be happy,
I have fading blonde hair,
Like the sun at dusk,
I have bright blue eyes,
That make me rise,
Halloween's my type,
I can't wait for the hype,
Singing and dancing I sure like to do,
Maybe I could do it along with you,
I have an older brother,
And a loving mother,
A father who cares and who shares,
This.
Is.
Me.

Poppy Guest (9)
Copmanthorpe Primary School, Copmanthorpe

This Is Me!

Hi, my name is Evie,
And I like shopping,
I play tennis with my dad,
But when I lose, I get mad!
At times I am naughty,
But mostly very sporty.
I love watermelon,
I could eat it all day!
I go for long walks with my mum,
And dad.
I love drawing,
This is me!

Evie Appleton (10)
Copmanthorpe Primary School, Copmanthorpe

You Can Find Me

I might be slow,
But I make up for a sliding tackle.
I don't know what position I am,
But you can find me on the pitch.

My grandpa,
He likes a lot of different flavours.
I don't like pie,
But I like eating big breakfasts.

I am dyslexic.
That makes me different from everyone else.
I am smart in my own way,
But you can find me working hard.

I love a lot of video games.
Fortnite is my favourite.
I also like Monopoly and board games,
But you can find me with my Lego.

Henry Shaw (10)
Dovedale Primary School, Long Eaton

My Favourite Sport

F ootball people know and love.

O thers like different sports over other sports, football, basketball, or tennis.

O thers may agree or not but it is their opinion so they're not wrong.

T hat football can be hard but other sports are too.

B ut matches can be hard, easy, or easy and hard.

A nything can be hard, easy, or both in football.

L ove for football is reigning in my passion and heart.

L ove for football from me is blazing through my heart.

Oscar Bailey (9)

Dovedale Primary School, Long Eaton

The Sportsman

I am going to be a phenomenal batsman
And an outstanding bowler
Don't try to get past me
Or it will be fire on the pitch
This is me!
I will be an excellent centre-attacking midfielder
I will be a good possessive midfielder
I will also be a good passer, shooter and have
good physicality

Now I'm retired, I achieved what I wanted to
And now I'm rich so now I will donate
Some of the money to charity
And to family
This is me!

Sahil Avasthy (9)
Dovedale Primary School, Long Eaton

Animals

I am an animal expert.
Ask me any question about animals and I'll know the answer.

Yesterday I impressed my friends about capybaras.
Did you know they are the largest rodent?

Today I wowed my teacher about Rothschild giraffes.
Did you know they don't have spots below their knees?

Tomorrow I will amaze my mum and dad about sloths.
Did you know there are two types, the three-toed and two-toed?

This is me.

Noah Mitchell (9)
Dovedale Primary School, Long Eaton

Just About Me

I like going to school,
Games, friends and powering tools!

My sister likes her phone,
Her snacks, her teddies, and her zone.

I like to drink,
Eat, ride, and blink.

My sister likes to play on the playground (not the school one),
Riding her bike at the playground too!

I like my pet blankets,
They snooze, they sleep, oh and they just love to relax!

Harrison Sage (10)
Dovedale Primary School, Long Eaton

This Is Me

L oved by my family and friends

A mazing, I'm the amazing one

Y esterday I came to school

L adybirds are very friendly to me, flying in the sky

A rt is me, I love art

R ight, you got it right

O rganisation, I'm very organised

S uper, you're so super

E motional, I get very emotional.

Layla Rose Day (9)

Dovedale Primary School, Long Eaton

My Best Friends!

I have two best friends
They're the best
Our friendship is never going to end!
This is me
I'm happy because of them
We have the best sleepovers
I bet they're better than yours!
This is me
I hope we go to the same secondary school
Even though we live quite far from each other
Everyone loves us because we're cool!

Lilly Dudley (10)
Dovedale Primary School, Long Eaton

This Is Me

I'm hard work, I'm smart
One day, I will be an author
Encouraged to read
Writing and writing, I enjoy writing.

I'm running, I'm scoring
One day I'll be a footballer
Scoring and scoring
Until the world is glorious and loving.

I love past
I love steak
One day, I'll be a chef
Cooking.

Andrei Florescu (10)
Dovedale Primary School, Long Eaton

My Favourite Things To Do

These are some of my favourite things to do
This is me!

I enjoy reading, it's so much fun!
More relaxing than maths
I can't even do a sum!
This is me!

Baking is the best, but when I love making food
But when it burns I get in a mood!
This is me!

Art is great, but I'm not the best
It always makes a mess
This is me!

Bethan James (9)
Dovedale Primary School, Long Eaton

Me

L uca loves gaming, it's his time to shine
U nder the bed, he plays
C ats surrounding him he just doesn't care
A t the TV he stares

A fine gamer indeed
Soon he'll be seen
This is me.

Luca Needham (9)
Dovedale Primary School, Long Eaton

Food!

I like my food
I like my sweet stuff
I sit on the sofa
With my food
Munching away
I love it way too much
I will never let it go
Because it's so darn good!

Food!

Blake Hamblett (9)
Dovedale Primary School, Long Eaton

Furry Foxes

F lyaway fox,

O ften stealing belongings,

X -ray vision for hunting chickens,

E xecute the chicken,

S leeping through the day.

Jayden Tavernor (9)

Dovedale Primary School, Long Eaton

This Is Me

I will stay a crazy person,
This will always be the version,
I'm also fun and kind,
With a super creative mind,
I am a very silly person as you can see,
That's why I'm writing all about me.

I'm passionate about singing and all about sports,
I have a lot to offer on the basketball courts,
I'm in the school choir, I can sing the highest note,
When I open my mouth, my voice always floats.

When I walk down the corridor, everyone says hi,
But by the end of Year 6, it will be hard to say
goodbye.

My favourite game is Truth or Dare, you could even
tell me to fight a bear,
I hope my words aren't tiring you,
Next time, you can write a poem all about you,
But until then, this is me!

Amelia Allen (11)
Downsview Primary School, Upper Norwood

How To Make A Rose

Ingredients:
A messy bedroom.
A cheeseburger.
100lb of fun.
20lb of adventures.
A dash of mischief.
Petals from a rose.

Now you need to:
Add 100lb of fun.
Mix in the cheeseburger.
Stir roughly, while adding 20lb of adventures.
Next, add a dash of mischief.
Sprinkle happiness into the mix.
Spread the mix neatly over a tray of baking paper.
Cook until crispy and smooth.
Coat the whole mix in petals from the two roses
and let it cool down for an hour.
Voila, you have created me!
This is how I am!

Rose Stewart (9)
Downsview Primary School, Upper Norwood

This Is Me

I am the girl who cheers kids up,
I am a big hugger,
I am as cute as a baby,
I am as pretty as a baby,
I am a big smiler,
I am loving,
I am willing,
I am positive,
I am cheerful,
I am daring,
I am smart,
I am energetic,
I am hard-working,
I am fun to play with,
I am independent,
I am lovely,
I am friendly,
I am caring,
I am strong,
I am passionate,
I am fearless,

I am crazy mad,
I am tall,
I am joyful,
This is me... Iman.

Iman

Downsview Primary School, Upper Norwood

Riddle Me?

I have black hair as dark as night.

I like doing abstract paintings

I always draw pandas!

I like repetitive rhymes

I will always help someone when they're sad.

I never ever give up even if the wall of worries is too high up.

I listen carefully to what people are saying.

I love poetry

But I have a chance to save the world someday I know I do definitely do.

Who am I?

: Lili Owen.

Lili Owen (10)

Downsview Primary School, Upper Norwood

This Is Me

I am a...
Fun dancer,
Nice swimmer,
Happy cellist,
Story teller,
Confident artist,
Wild singer,
Proud footballer,
Curious cleaner,
Respectful student,
Funny friend,
Silly baker,
Loving person,
Marvellous predictor,
This is me, Megan.

Megan
Downsview Primary School, Upper Norwood

This Is Me

I am loved
I am strong
I am silly
I am a try hard
I am thin
I am small
I am friendly
I am amazing!
I am silly

This is me, Raabia.

Raabia
Downsview Primary School, Upper Norwood

Me

Good runner
Great cooker
Top gamer.

Leonardo Kim Sing (6)
Downsview Primary School, Upper Norwood

Untitled

I am as hyper as sugar,
I am as hungry as a seagull,
I am as confident as going into the woods on your own,
In the pitch dark.

I am as happy as a dog smiling,
I like football, I like Messi,
I like my scooter.

I especially like pro scooters,
I like my bike,
I like pro bikers.

Kole Dolan (9)
Fair Isle Primary School, Kirkcaldy

This Is Me And My Life

This is me,
I am happy. I am sad. I am angry,
When I am hot, I'm like a ball of fire,
I am great, I am brave. I am as strong as a
bodybuilder,
I am sleepy, I am tired, I am as wet as a river which
is flowing,
I am funny, I am fidgety, I am fun,
I am chilled, I am good at sports like football and
basketball,
I have pets called Apollo and Ted, I am friendly, I
am fearless,
I am playful, I am sparky,
I laugh, I am like a piece of cake,
I am creative,
I am English, I like exploring new things,
I am a swimmer,
My birthday is January 9th,
I am as happy as a bunny.

George Chisnall (9)
Heamoor Community Primary School, Heamoor

This Is Me

This is me
I am friendly, messy and kind
I can sometimes be
Moody, angry and sad
But that's just me.

Jasmine Elverstone (13)
Heath Lane Academy, Earl Shilton

All About Me

My name is Taqweem
Sometimes I can be a bit mean
I have just turned ten
I like to go to London to see Big Ben

I like to explore
I would love to learn a lot more
Sometimes I can be twisting and turning
With a lot of emotions running wild

The only way to stop the anger
Is to blow it away
This won't happen again today
As I will gently blow it away.

Taqweem Hassan (10)
Heathrow Primary School, Sipson

Emaan's Ramadan

R amadan is the best

A feast of yummy meal on a loud party.

M y presents are cute, I have ice cream after mosque.

A t night, we have fireworks, the fireworks are cool.

D ay, we go out to a fun place, we go everywhere.

A t our house, we have so much fun with family.

N ight is so cool, we do puzzles. They are fun puzzles

Emaan Bilal (7)

Heathrow Primary School, Sipson

Football

F ootball is my hobby.

O utside, is where I play football.

O n the grass, I love to kick the ball.

T urn around and put your hand up at the end of lunchtime.

B e kind to everyone on the pitch.

A lways be amazing on the pitch.

L ove playing football.

L ove being kind on the pitch.

Daksh Devasi (7)

Heathrow Primary School, Sipson

This Is Me

I am sunny
And extremely funny
I am a little shy
And I hate flies
I am hyper
And I am a good typer
I am calm
And I hate alarms
I am very loving
And I don't know how to use an oven
I am always brave
And I know how to behave
I am nice
And I hate mice.

Harriet Coughlan (9)
Heathrow Primary School, Sipson

All About Me

I am a...
Animal lover,
Chocolate eater,
Sweet tooth,
Spring wisher,
Flee from spiders,
Keen swimmer,
Energetic power,
Insects are gross,
English is my weak point,
I am very shy,
And finally,
A good helper.

Phoebe Whitehead-Collins (10)
Heathrow Primary School, Sipson

Dinah's Food Poem

D elicious chicken nuggets are my favourite.

I like ice cream.

N o more chocolate because I have too much.

A pples are healthy and sweet.

H appy is how I feel when I am painting.

Dinah Umair (7)

Heathrow Primary School, Sipson

Banee

B eing happy,

A lways calm and excited,

N ervous to talk to other people,

E xcited to learn,

E very day I like to listen to music.

Banee Dhutti (9)

Heathrow Primary School, Sipson

Divraj

Divraj is a furious
Tired person
And a hard-working
Young boy.

Divraj is a car-loving
Kind, caring friend
And I am shy when a guest comes.

Divraj Sidhu (9)
Heathrow Primary School, Sipson

Eighty-One Words About Me And My Life!

Football, family, electronics and gymnastics
They're what make me fantastic.

Football when it rains
Even better in the sun
But it's always my favourite
Like my mum.

Electronics, electronics
All are fun
I use them all the time
Even when I'm with my mum.

My mum, my dad, I love them so bad
I have them in my life
I am so glad.

Gymnastics on Thursday
Wish it was every day
We've learned so much since the start of last year.

Nevaeh Renee Lawrence (10)
High Crags Primary Leadership Academy, Shipley

All About Me!

I am...
Bored
Crazy
Lazy
Friendly
Annoying
Sleepy
Creative
Not very intelligent
And lastly, I am very overwhelming
Sometimes!

Arya Field (10)
High Crags Primary Leadership Academy, Shipley

Dogs

To make me you will need:
A dust-filled bedroom
A pinch of powder
100lbs of cats and dogs
A mouthful of paper
A pinch of a dog
A dash of Chevrolet
A pinch of a pig.

Eli Webb (8)
Horrington Primary School, West Horrington

What Sport Am I?

I wear gloves to save balls so my hands don't hurt,
I wear boots with studs,
I kick balls high to the other side,
I kick penalty shots,
I save goals,
I kick balls into goals,
I kick free kicks,
I drink at half-time to get energy,
I go home at full time,
I play matches,
We get sent off if we get a red card,
We get a warning if we get a yellow card.

Answer: Football.

Ryley-Mclaren Howard (9)
Hungerford Primary School, Hungerford

This Is Me

F ast runner

L ittle aggressive

E xample for some

X -ray artist

I am me!

B ut...

L earning-struggler

E xam-passer

This is me!

Casey Scarlett (9)
Hungerford Primary School, Hungerford

All About Me

K icking a football

A favourite rapper is Xsontol okay.

D ad is great at football like me.

E ating Domino's is my favourite takeaway.

W WE is my favourite game.

I like doing sit-ups.

L ike ICS games.

S ometimes I play my PlayStation.

O range juice.

N inja Turtles are my favourite.

Kade Wilson (8)

Kirkshaws Primary School, Coatbridge

Who I Am

M y dog's name is Oskar.

A mbitious - I want to be a star.

D azzling smile.

D elightful.

I like ice cream.

S o, my favourite singer is Taylor Swift.

O rdinary eight-year-old.

N ice to everyone.

Maddison McGraw (8)

Kirkshaws Primary School, Coatbridge

All About Me

R especting everyone who is talking
E veryone is important
U sing my artistic skills
B roccoli is my favourite vegetable
E veryone has something they are good at
N ever give up.

Reuben Kennedy (9)

Kirkshaws Primary School, Coatbridge

All About Me!

I am a child with brown hair and hazel eyes,
When I go to the chippy I get a pie,
I love to read,
When it comes to teamwork I like to take the lead.

I am very messy but yet so friendly,
But sometimes I feel lonely,
I love to play hockey
But I am never cocky.

I like to be sporty,
I hope I still am when I am forty,
I laugh and giggle all the time
And I like to eat a lime.

Georgia Purkis (10)
Lea St Mary's Catholic Primary School, Preston

What Makes Me, Me!

Hi, my name is Dante Lewis,
I know that I can do it,
I wake up from my sleep
With a bounce, a jump and a leap!

I have a brother whose name is Dane,
Sometimes he's a pain,
With a boom, I leave the room,
With the slowest kind of zoom.

School is kind of bad,
Mondays make me sad,
I'm the best I can be,
So that's what makes me, me!

Dante Lewis (10)

Lea St Mary's Catholic Primary School, Preston

Emmy

E nthusisastic, loves playing with my friends, loves playing with my dog and loves my family!

M arvellous at drawing, loves painting and making some Halloween art with my friends and family.

M ostly loves travelling and going on planes with my family, travelling is fun!

Y oung and a really enthusiastic artist. Art is my hobby.

Emmy Macdonald (9)

Locharbriggs Primary School, Locharbriggs

Cory

C ory loves playing competitive football and playing against people with his friends.

O ptimistic, kind and caring.

R eally good at video games.

Y oung and fit and good at football.

Cory Fraser (9)

Locharbriggs Primary School, Locharbriggs

Jamie

J amie is my name.
A lways loves to hang out with friends.
M aths is the best.
I love bugs and frogs.
E nergetic and likes to play football with Peter, Jai and Cory.

Jamie Saunders (9)

Locharbriggs Primary School, Locharbriggs

Halloween

H alloween is the best
A ll of it is better than the rest
L oving it when you see scary costumes
L oving it when they hand out perfumes
O ut in the dark!
W hen all of it is scary and sharp
E ven if it's too dark for the park
E ven though it's too dark
N ever forget about the Halloween night!

Murren Manning (11)
Loretto RC Primary School, Musselburgh

Untitled

I am so happy all the time
And all my friends call me
Flavioski lil broski and I like to use technology.
I play Roblox and Minecraft!
Oh yeah! Oh yeah!
Gaming on the couch
And snacking on tacos.
Oh yeah! Oh yeah!
Snacking on tacos
Calling on the couch
With Jacob and Matty
Oh yeah! Oh yeah!

Flavio Ccarlo (11)
Loretto RC Primary School, Musselburgh

About Me

First, I'm a good listener.
Second, I'm a good person for helping.
Third, I'm loving and caring.
Fourth, I'm a funny person if you're sad.
Fifth, I love maths and I'm pretty good at it.
Sixth, I'm clumsy and a bit stupid.
Seventh, I'm a good friend to play with.
Eighth, I am good to new people and kind.
Finally, my unfunny jokes are funny.

Reggie Martin (9)
Merriott Primary School, Merriott

This Is Me

Q ueen

U nder the colourful umbrella

I guanas are green

N ice boy

N ice cold ice cream.

Quinn Brander-Stark (8)

Newberries Primary School, Radlett

This Is Me

J elly wobbles.
A pples fall on the floor, *crash!*
E lephants like stomping super loud!

Jaejah Sullivan (8)
Newberries Primary School, Radlett

This Is Me

T ough as a bull, a bulldozer or a wrecking ball,
H elpful as a teacher,
I nterested in football, you need to be fast,
S illy as a baby and a monkey too.

I am as funny as can be,
S porty as Mr Furse.

M emories are my favourite things,
E ncouraging people to work and play.

Oscar Morrison (8)

North Petherton Community Primary School, North
Petherton

This Is Me!

T eaching kids like me is fun,
H undreds of children having great times,
I 'm as smart as a teacher,
S upportive people all around.

I love outside so, so much,
S inging birds are so much fun.

M angoes and pineapples are so yummy,
E ating carrots and bananas.

Holly Davis (7)

North Petherton Community Primary School, North
Petherton

This Is Me!

T he best game is Toca Life World

H arry is my name, bro

I 'm as hungry as a lion

S wimming is my favourite sport

I drink tea and eat biscuits every Monday

S anta is the kindest person on Earth

M y best friend is Noah J

E ly is my best friend.

Harry Lloyd (7)

North Petherton Community Primary School, North Petherton

This Is Me!

T rying my best,

H igh hopes and delightful dreams, like candyfloss clouds,

I n the pool, I splash, play

S eeing the future in the sky.

I n my dreams superheroes pop up,

S aving the day, did you proud.

M y name is,

E dith.

Edith Court (7)

North Petherton Community Primary School, North Petherton

This Is Me

T -rex is a giant

H appy kitten in a house

I can roll in a field for a long time

S neaky as a serpent.

I draw like an artist

S illy as my kitten.

M unch on a pear

E xcellent elephant.

Elliott Jones (7)

North Petherton Community Primary School, North Petherton

A Recipe For My Dog, Marshall

Add a pinch of kindness and nice
Pour in some nice and sweetness
Blend nice and kind and more nice
Then warm.
That's my dog.

Suraya Kamara (9)
Peel Primary School, Eliburn East

This Is Me

I'm an animal lover, dogs are so cool,
I love playing netball with my friends in school.
I'm great at gymnastics,
It's truly fantastic.

My eyes are green emeralds sparkling in the sky,
I love climbing trees and going up so high.
I love tumbling and flipping every day,
When I'm with my cousin, time flies away.

I'm as skinny as a branch and as short as a bug,
When I eat food I'm as slow as a slug.
I love swimming, I'm like a fish,
If it's in front of me I'll eat any dish.

I'm kind and friendly to everyone I meet,
I love chocolate, it's so tasty to eat.
Art, art and more art please,
As rapid as a tiger, I have very fast knees.

Isabella Patrick (11)

Pencoed Primary School, Pencoed

This Is Me!

To create me, you will need:
First, add a pinch of cheekiness to make me mischievous.
Two tablespoons of adult humour so I can understand jokes you probably don't!
Put in a teaspoon of taste in memes, so I know how to make you laugh if you're feeling down.
Add five sprinkles of being a bookworm.
Add in three pinches of silliness so I can make you laugh and giggle and have a good time
Add seven drops of undiluted sour orange juice and then some sweet, sweet blackberry juice so I'm sweet but also sour and tangy with two different sides.
Now add 150ml of kindness, respect and maturity so I'm not too silly.
And finally, add a nice freshly-made hot chocolate (with marshmallows) to warm me up.

Now you will need to:
Put the kindness, respect and maturity into a bowl with being a bookworm, adult humour and a warm, new, freshly-made hot chocolate.

Mix it up and then pour it into a roasty, toasty pan heated on a stove.

Now, get your sweet and sour squash and pour it into the mix and wait until it starts to pop and fizz.

Now, get your pinch of cheekiness... But wait, we're still not done!

Next, pop in the taste of memes so I can make you smile and laugh and you'll be as small as a tiny giraffe on the floor dying of laughter.

Then, mix it up with the 150ml of warm water from a cup.

Add it to the bubbling, fizzing, fun-filled pan.

Then you must wait five minutes if you can.

Then mix it up with a whisk in the nice warm pan.

Now, we're nearly done!

Add six pinches of being the youngest child into the bowl and mix it up before it goes cold.

Add it to the pan and *wazam!* You've created me.

This is me!

Clara Curtis (9)

Pencoed Primary School, Pencoed

This Is Me: My Recipe

Ingredients:

Water because every recipe has water, right?

An energy drink to make it crazy

A bowl to put it in

A spoon to mix and stir like crazy

A microwave to melt the ingredients

Sweets and chocolate so it tastes amazing!

Sprinkles and edible glitter so it's very sparkly like a rainbow and gives it magic!

Squirty cream.

Now you will need to:

1. First, you need to add water and energy drinks to make it crazy like a hyena!

2. Now, you need to mix so crazily that your arms fall off!

3. Add chocolate and sweets to make it as sweet as honey.

4. *Melt it all!*

5. Now, add Mentos and Coke to make it fizz, pop, bang and sparkle like Bonfire Night.

6. Stir real good so it swirls like a tornado.

7. Finally, add squirty cream, edible glitter and rainbow sprinkles so it's magic!

Zara Jones (9)

Pencoed Primary School, Pencoed

This Is Me

To make me, you will need:
A touch of madness
A block of chocolate
A tablespoon of loudness
A pinch of laughter
A bowl of focus
Five sweets.

Now you will need to:
First, add a block of chocolate to make me sweet and lovely like a bowl of delicious sugar.
Then add a touch of madness to make me a mad monkey when I play.
Next, mix in a tablespoon of loudness because I'm a loud ferocious lion when I speak.
After, add 10lb of laughter so I can laugh and giggle like a crazy clown.
Also, add five sweets to make me as energetic as a wild puppy in the garden.
Lastly, gently sprinkle in a bowl of focus because I need to be as focused as a huge eagle hunting its quick, sly prey.

Sophia Davies (10)
Pencoed Primary School, Pencoed

I Am Different

I am Isabella and Isabella is me.

A nd I love my family, friends and animals.

M y favourite animal is a liger, yes, it is real!

D eep, dark ocean doesn't scare me!

I love Warrior Cats, it's my favourite game and book.

F ootball, cross-country and netball are what I like to do.

F alling from heights is what scares me the most!

E nergy is what I have lots of.

R ight now, my favourite food is spaghetti Bolognese.

E very time I go to the beach, I go bodyboarding.

N ow last but not least, my favourite colour is blue.

T his is me!

Isabella Evans (10)

Pencoed Primary School, Pencoed

This Is Me!

To create me, you will need:
Ten sweets
A bit of flour
15 bars of chocolate
10lb of sugar
A dash of brightness
A bit of cake
And a sprinkle of happiness.

Now you need to:
First, you have to add ten sweets to make me crazy.
Next, you have to add a bit of flour to make me sassy.
Then, add 15 bars of chocolate to make me smile.
Next, add a piece of cake to quiet me down.
Then, add 10lb of fun and mischief.
Next, you have to spread the mix neatly over a tray of baking paper.

After this, cook until it is glazed and bubbles come out.
Finally, sprinkle some happiness and wait until it cools down.

Ruby Hancock (9)

Pencoed Primary School, Pencoed

This Is Me!

I am nice!
I am caring for my family,
I have a nice, beautiful best friend,
I am a super sporty star,
This is me!

I am me!
My hair's like caramel dripping in the sun,
My eyes are beautiful blue balls of sapphires,
My smile's as beautiful as a rose,
This is me!

I am sad!
I get anxious by loud annoying noises,
My dogs make me happy when I feel down,
Sometimes my sister drives me up the wall,
This is me!

I am kind
I am mad
I am loving
I am grumpy

I am bored
I am a good helper
This is me!

Bella Gill (10)
Pencoed Primary School, Pencoed

Ingredients For Me

First, you will need a brain filled with footballs.
Second, you will need a stomach filled with chicken.
Third, you will need ankles made of chocolate.
Next, you will need legs of steel.

First, add the bouncy football and juicy chicken into a gigantic glass bowl.
Next, mix the Dairy Milk chocolate with the rusty steel.
Now, add the mushy sour sweets.
Then add the five strawberry acai.
Mix all the ingredients together like a witch and cauldron.
Tap with a wand-shaped spoon - *Abracadabra!*
Abracadabra, it's done.

This is me.

Oliver Jones (10)
Pencoed Primary School, Pencoed

This Is Me

P layful like a puppy eating its treats

O ver the moon like an astronaut

P opcorn professional when I eat popcorn, I am a crazy person

P laying Fortnite like a pro

Y our best friend is caring like a mother bear

A lways hungry like a seagull in the summer

N ever give up, I am determined like a shark catching its prey

N aughty like a monkey stealing a banana from its mother

E vil mind like a devil.

Poppy Burgess (9)

Pencoed Primary School, Pencoed

This Is Me

T alking all the time
H appiness everywhere you look
I s as funny as a cheeky monkey
S assy as a cat walking alone on the street

I s as loud as a chimpanzee making fun of a human
S leepy as a sloth on the school run

M ental like a puppy when its owner arrives
E njoys dancing.

Seren-Jade Gilboy (10)

Pencoed Primary School, Pencoed

This Is Me

M y favourite place is the beach, I swim like a
dolphin

I like the colour blue, like the sky and the sea

A mazing day and night

B eing kind and helpful

E legant as a bird and a swan

L oud as a tiger and a lion

L akes are my favourite place, I like to swim like a
swan

A rt is my favourite.

Mia-Bella Porter (9)

Pencoed Primary School, Pencoed

This Is Me

E fficient at rugby
T ough as a rock
H elpful and curious
A rtist when drawing
N oisy like a baby monkey

F ortnite gamer; better than Ninja in his prime
O bvious when answering questions
R ages when gaming
D efensive when playing football.

Ethan Ford (9)
Pencoed Primary School, Pencoed

This Is Me

T ough as a rock

H orrific at tennis

I 'm like a giraffe

S nakes are my biggest fear

I 'll die without a drink

S uper strong like a lion

M y legs are going to fall off when I run too much

E xcellent at rugby and scoring tries.

Will Powell (10)

Pencoed Primary School, Pencoed

This Is Me

T all as a bear
H ot as fire
I 'm feisty when I go to bed
S ometimes I feel like I'm on top of the world

I 'm as cold as ice cream
S harp as a knife

M agnificent mind
E veryone is special.

Freya Beckinsale (10)

Pencoed Primary School, Pencoed

This Is Me

I am good like Ronaldo with a ball
I hope that I get very tall
I have blue eyes like a blue sea
I don't like to eat peas
I like cricket a bit
I like oranges, peaches and grapes
I like grapes and ships
I like to tap my apple
I like pure water.

Lucas Austin (10)
Pencoed Primary School, Pencoed

Sophie May

S miling like always

O utside lover

P reparing for school

H ungry as a horse

I ndependent worker

E nergy always up

M arvellous mischief

A lways approachable

Y ou will love me.

Sophie Oliver (9)

Pencoed Primary School, Pencoed

I Am Me

I ncredible impatience

A mazing artist
M cDonald's muncher

M agnificent mathematician
E xcellent explorer!

Harrison Coburn (10)
Pencoed Primary School, Pencoed

This Is Me

I am a spider,
I am a football player,
I like school,
I like maths,
I like Minecraft,
I am as furry as a dog,
I like my home,
This is me!

Brandon Brandon (10)
Pencoed Primary School, Pencoed

I Am A...

I am a...
Art maker
Football player
Winter wisher
Pasta eater
Elephant lover
Anxious reader
And finally...
I am me!

Tillie Lovell (10)
Pencoed Primary School, Pencoed

Untitled

C hristmas is the best time of the year,

H appy times of the year.

R onnie

I am from England

S haring with the family

T he apple was nice

M um and Dad

A rsenal is the best

S ports, my favourite sports are football, boxing and golf.

Ronnie Van der Merwe (9)

Petersfield CE (A) Primary School, Orwell

Untitled

As I start training
The breeze makes it raining
The ball travels through my feet
And the food makes me weak,
With a smack of the glove
The ball has gone above.

Leo Alexander (10)
Petersfield CE (A) Primary School, Orwell

Beatrice

B rave
E nergetic
A mazing
T errific
R ebel
I mportant
C aring
E xcited.

Beatrice McKenzie (10)
Petersfield CE (A) Primary School, Orwell

All About Me!

I am Daisy! My favourite colour is teal.
I love to feel happy.
When I'm sad my cat makes me feel better
Although I do not like it when he sits on my
favourite mat.
My best friend is Lily.
I have blonde hair and blue/green eyes.
I like to read and like to put beads on strings.
I have a nice and kind mum, dad and sister.
My favourite weather is a rainbow because
I love all the colours in it.

Daisy Hardy (10)
Prenton Primary School, Prenton

About Me

I am as funny as a clown
I am as sweet as honey
I shine as bright as a star
I am fast like a cheetah
I am busy as a bee

What makes me me?
What makes me special? What makes me happy?
What makes me funny? What makes me smile?
What makes me kind?

About me!
My name is Olivia I am kind, special and nice
If you wanna be my friend, just ask me
Of course I will say yes!

Olivia Morrell (10)
Prenton Primary School, Prenton

Absolutely Me

S mart

A mazing

M agnificent

U nique

E xcellent

L ovely

D elightful

U ndefeatable

N ever gives up

N ifty

I maginative

N eat

G rateful.

Samuel Dunning (8)

Prenton Primary School, Prenton

Acrostic Poem

B lamtastic
E xcellent
N ice

D aring
U nique
N ifty
N ever give up
I maginative
N eat
G reat.

Ben Dunning (9)

Prenton Primary School, Prenton

My Hair

My hair is a soft, glowing picture for everyone to see.

Swish, swoosh! goes my cool hair.

My hair is the moonlight in the dark and sunlight in the brightness.

My hair makes me shine in the spotlight.

My hair is the spotlight, spotlight, spotlight.

My hair is a fresh, free haircut.

When my hair looks at the sun it screams drumbeats.

My hair is like a person playing an instrument.

My hair makes me, me.

Kamal Owolabi (8)

Rathfern Primary School, London

This Is Me

I am a superstar striker.
I am the best friend.
I have the best family.
Pepperoni pizza is yummy for me.
This is me.

Santino Abbey (7)

Rillington Community Primary School, Rillington

Johnny's Poem

My name is Johnny Morgun
And I am in Year 3
My favourite thing to eat is pizza for my tea
I also like to play football with my friends
If I get time, I like to build a den.

Johnny Morgun (7)
Rothley CE Primary Academy, Rothley

Rhyme About My Friend

My name is Roo
I am twenty-two
My favourite colour is blue
This is the colour for me and you.

Oliver Reid
Rothley CE Primary Academy, Rothley

Myself

M y name is Joan and I am nine years old
Y ou should always be yourself
S aying kind words is a way of showing kindness
E veryone is to be treated equally
L ove everyone because Jesus loves you
F orever we are God's people.

One last thing we are all children of God
And we should behave like the good samaritan
Who helped an injured Jewish man

So be kind and be yourself
We are all unique.

Joan Ejakpovi (9)
Sacred Heart Catholic Primary School, Middlesbrough

Me

I am Norah
I am seven
I am nice, I am friendly
Would you like to join me
On a new adventure?

I am as sweet as a cupcake
I am a golden star
Eyes like chocolate
Hair like tar

Smart as an owl
Brave as a lion
Smooth like butter
Rubbing my mistakes

Look out
Here I come
I am marching
Down to the beat
I drum
I am brave

I am good
I take no apologies
This is me

Marching to the sun
I am a fireball
Here I come
I am a warrior
Yeah, that's what I'll become

Look out, you're breaking
Down to dust
Don't make me angry
I'll be a monster
Here I come
I'm stomping on everyone
Pay no attention
That is perfection
Despicable
Unstoppable.

Norah Sibi (7)
Sacred Heart Catholic Primary School, Middlesbrough

All About Me And You

I love to do something with you every day with a
smile on my face.
After school, in the pool, I love to have a go at
floating in a cool pool.
I like to go get ice cream after a sunny, hot day
with a sprinkle of joy and a dash of happiness.
Full of new feelings we watch the sun set and fall
asleep safe and sound in our beds under the stars
far ahead.
My pillow is as soft as silk and smells like butterfly
milk.
All of us are sweet or sour depending on the hour.
Before I rise I think of all the lovely things that
have happened in my life
And amongst all those lovely things is you.
Remember that friendship never stops growing.
We are all happy and safe in this peaceful little
world full of goodness.

Aaliyah Jones (9)
Shavington Primary School, Shavington

This Is Me

My dog's name is Bobby.

He is cute, he is as small as a flute.

He is fluffy.

He's as soft as a teddy.

He is two and never gets the flu.

And when he does there's really nothing you can do.

But when I feel bad I say, "What's up lad? You okay?"

What's your favourite letter because mine is A!

Now on to me...

When I'm sad I might get mad but only for a while.

And when I calm down

I say, "I wish I could touch the sky and say winner, winner chicken dinner"

Then a bit more of my dog...

He will lick you and put his tongue all over you!

I let him because I don't mind.

It's because I'm kind you'll find!

Archie Clark-Owen (7)

Shavington Primary School, Shavington

This Is My Day

Let me tell you about my day,
I only got a couple of things to say.
When I wake up I am very tired
But it only lasts for some hours.
I arrive at school.
Some days rule but some days drool
Because I have this thing inside
That comes out when I cry.
It's like fire.
It burns and it always twists and turns.
Sometimes it shoots but I will never give a doubt.
When it is like fire I am called Scary
But when it dies down I go back to playing fairies.
I think this is the end
I hope this sends!

Poppy Carney (9)
Shavington Primary School, Shavington

This Is Me

My dog is the love of my life
But her bark is as sharp as a knife.

I love to do gymnastics and also flick
And I love to show off my tricks.

Pizza is my favourite but I know it's unhealthy
But I am still stealthy.

Daisies are my favourite because they're pretty...
Why won't my mum let me get a kitty?

Hearts are my favourite shape,
Maybe I should go get a cake.

I do lots of competitions, and I've got one gold,
Maybe that's why I can fold.

Arlia Fayers (9)
Shavington Primary School, Shavington

Who Am I?

I have long black hair.
My friend loves to play with me.
I am cheerful and kind.
I love dodgeball.
I love swimming, it is so calm.
As pretty as a dog.
I love my family.
I love gymnastics, especially handstands and cartwheels.
I love Stitch.
As cheerful as a dolphin.
I am kind.
Who am I?

Savannah Pourawal (7)
Shavington Primary School, Shavington

This Is Me

I always dress up quite nicely.
Come to the dance floor,
You'll be amazed when your eyes meet me!
I have a good sense of humour
And I'm so nice I'll never spread a rumour.
I dress with glam but I really like ham.
I love glitter although I need a sitter.
This is me!

Eliza Randle (8)
Shavington Primary School, Shavington

Who Am I?

I have long blonde hair.
I have pink bunny ears.
I've got a cardigan.
I'm a female.
I wear Doc Martens and grey tights.
My shirt is as white as a cloud.
I wear a black skirt.
I also have glasses and love reading books.

Ivy Banks (8)
Shavington Primary School, Shavington

This Is Me

Me and Mic never let go of the rope.
Me and the cats are best friends forever.
If I let go of them they will cry forever.
I'm the fastest in my class.
I can outrun them all.
If you need me, just give me a call.
This is me!

Lillia Phillips (8)
Shavington Primary School, Shavington

This Is Me

I am a Pokémon card collector.
I am as funny as Magikarp.
I'm unique like Arceus.
I am like Miraidon.
My favourite Pokémon card is Ohio created by me
And I also like to watch Charizard on TV.

William Jasinski (9)
Shavington Primary School, Shavington

This Is Me

I am a...
Animal lover
Meat eater
TV watcher
Summer wisher
Nutella maker
Dog/cat lover
Gymnastics lover
Sanrio lover
Drawing lover
And finally...
A kind helper.

Kimmy Li (9)
Shavington Primary School, Shavington

Who Am I?

I have curly hair.
I am kind and polite to my brother and other
people when they are worried and scared.
My favourite thing to do is go to Primark to get
Stitch things.
Who am I?

Poppy Wood (7)
Shavington Primary School, Shavington

This Is My Life

I am a...
Wasp killer
Chocolate eater
Book lover
Night owl
Hoodie lover
Dance maker
Early riser
And finally, a craft lover
This is me.

Sasha Pourawal (10)
Shavington Primary School, Shavington

Who Am I?

My hair is as shiny as the sun.
I have a tall, straight body.
I have a short fringe.
I have big feet.
I wear cute or smart clothes every day.
Who am I?

Isabella Thompson-Edge (7)
Shavington Primary School, Shavington

Who Am I?

I have brown eyes
And I also have black hair.
I am very good at football.
I really like football
And I also like scoring goals.
Who am I?

Lucas Li (7)
Shavington Primary School, Shavington

This Is Me

Perfect at Dad's.
Watch me dodge your jabs.
Head in books.
Good at hitting a beat.
This is me!

Brody Xennon Steele (8)

Shavington Primary School, Shavington

Ice Cream

I love ice cream
C an I get ice cream?
E xcited to get ice cream

C an I get a lot of ice cream?
R ed ice cream
E xcited to get red ice cream
A new ice cream
M y room is all ice cream and pink.

Limar Ahmad (9)
Simonside Community Primary School, Newcastle Upon Tyne

Me

I am a...
Coffee maker
Dog lover
Puppy hugger
Mushroom liker
Pizza giver
Writing hater
Swimming lover
Teacher helper
And finally...
I am a...
Groovy dancer.

Lilly Rae (10)

Simonside Community Primary School, Newcastle Upon Tyne

My Mum And Dad

My mum is amazing because she always cares for
me and loves me
And my dad's the same
He always cares for me and loves me
And on the weekend, we go on fun trips
Or play fun board games
On Saturdays, I go to a Polish school for now
But soon, I'm going to go fully
But first, they have to call my mum
When I need help, one of my parents always helps
me
My family is religious and on the weekends
We laugh, dance and talk
I love my family.

Natalia Tanska (9)
Spalding St Paul's Primary School, Spalding

Fantastic Gymnastic

A little girl called Elsie,
Who was nicknamed Smelsie,
Dreamed to be in competitions,
She had so much ambition.

Her dad thought she should be a part of gymnastic
And Elsie and her mum thought it would be
fantastic.

So off alone she went and became a gymnast;
Up in stages she went and four medals she got.

It all came with a smile and hopes for a trial
To be in the team
Because that's my dream!

Elsie Purvis (7)
Spalding St Paul's Primary School, Spalding

My Opposites

I love friends; I hate bullies.
I like playing; I dislike arguing.

I feel happy when in the sun.
I feel sad when I'm alone.

I like to go fast on my bike; I like to go slow on my scooter.
There is light in the day; it's dark at night.

Toby Waltham (8)
Spalding St Paul's Primary School, Spalding

This Is Me

Hi, I'm Nicole I'm so okay.
I love dragons and I've got a new game.
It's a football PS3 game called FIFA 23.
My sister also has a horse game.
I love puppies and dogs.
I am shy but my friends make me happy
And give me hugs when I go home.
I like drawing dragons because I'm an artist.
Yes 'm an artist okayay.
I have written stories, and poems at the end.

Nicole Szczepanski (10)
St Aidan's Primary School, Wishaw

I Will Love My Friend Forever

I love my friend, she's the best on every test
She is smart, that's my part.
Oh my friend makes me sleepy but
When I wake up she makes me happy.
If only I was friends with her forever
We could grow up, dance and sing together!
She is the only friend I'll ever have!
If she doesn't want to be my friend anymore
I'll be as sad as I was before!
This is me.

Simra Khan (7)
St Bernard's Catholic Primary School, Birmingham

The Girly Rap

I am kind
I am sweet
I am bright
I like to be neat
I like turquoise
Just like chalk white
Rainbows and unicorns
They're both the best
My teacher has a pet snake
It's a bit scary
My brother is annoying
He's a little crybaby
I have a friend called Sabah
Another called Huda
My name's Anaya Fatima
And I'm the best.

Anaya Fatima (8)
St Bernard's Catholic Primary School, Birmingham

This Is Who I Am

I am as kind as a butterfly.
I like flamingos because flamingos are pink
And pink is my favourite colour.
I am sweet as ice cream.
I like cats and kittens.
I like Huda, Mila, Minahil, Sabah, Alis and Fatmah.
I like kittens, cats and rabbits.
I like art.

Ruqaya Hussain (7)
St Bernard's Catholic Primary School, Birmingham

Ilayda's Acrostic Poem

I love dogs and my favourite breed is a Wiener-Dog

L oving, compassionate and generous

A pizza lover

Y ay, it's almost Friday

D ilara is so beautiful

A country that my cousins live in is Turkey and Ireland.

Ilayda Kaplan (9)

St Bernard's Catholic Primary School, Birmingham

This Is Me

I am...
A game player,
A social media fan,
A noodle eater,
A boost drinker,
A cat fan,
A TikToker,
A Snapchatter,
A times tables rockstar,
A Maher Zain fan,
A Naat fan,
A Netflixer,
A YouTuber,
A Kamarun fan.

Anya Noor Ali (8)
St Bernard's Catholic Primary School, Birmingham

Ibrahim

I play games on the PC
B lueberries taste good
R unning is fun and fast
A nd holidays are beautiful
H ot chicken is delicious
I sleep in bed to get my energy
M elons are also a good fruit.

Ibrahim Bahakam (7)

St Bernard's Catholic Primary School, Birmingham

Being Happy

I see a boy picking a cat up
I was happy and
I love ice cream, art, basketball and watching
football
I like pink
My crown is pink, like rose pink and
It is me
Ayesha Mohmand.

Ayesha Mohmand (8)
St Bernard's Catholic Primary School, Birmingham

This Is Me

A pples are nice
L ove my family
E xcited with my friends
E njoy playing Roblox
F riends are fun.

Aleef Aklaq (7)
St Bernard's Catholic Primary School, Birmingham

Zayan

Z ebras are fun
A rt is special
Y oghurt is delicious
A pples are crunchy
N ike shoes.

Zayan Ali
St Bernard's Catholic Primary School, Birmingham

Aayan

A pples

A rt is special

Y ou play hide-and-seek

A cting and singing

N ike shoes.

Muhammad Aayan (7)
St Bernard's Catholic Primary School, Birmingham

This Is Me

A drop of anger,
Three spoons of meanness,
A splat of kindness,
Put a pinch of annoyingness,
A piece of sweetness,
A drizzle of sadness,
A sprinkle of smelliness,
Finally, add a pinch of silliness.

Stir it nicely 100,000 times,
Put me in the baking pot,
Put me in the oven for a day,
Then you've made me.

Myan Patel (7)
St David's Prep School, Purley

This Is Me!

O ctober is my birth month,
C hinese is my culture,
T ogether we are best,
O utdoors is an adventure,
B aking is deliciously fun,
E lena is my name,
R ainbows make me happy.

Elena Wan (8)
St David's Prep School, Purley

All About Me!

I'm Neche, yeah, that's my name,
I really love my friends and family.
You like drawing? OMG same!
And I also like reading - well only slightly.

I love all things cute and pastel,
And the colours purple and turquoise.
If you need help, just give me a yell,
And I really love using my singing voice.

My favourite day is my birthday.
Handwriting, everyone always says mine is good.
Roblox is my favourite game to play,
And most of the time, I'm in a really happy mood.

Chinecherem Okafor (11)
St Helen's Primary School, Bishopbriggs

All About Me

T his is me, a Squishmallow collector
H aving fun is my favourite thing to do
I love animals, they are so cute
S now is my favourite weather, you can build a snowman

I have a pet hamster and two pet cats
S ausages are one of my favourite foods

M y cute hamster is called Hermione
E aster eggs are so chocolatey and yummy.

Lila Whitelaw (8)
St Helen's Primary School, Bishopbriggs

This Is Millie

Millie is my name
I am lovely, I am kind
I have a great mind
I'm as tall as a tree
I like to be as busy as a bee
And like to be as kind as can be
You'll always find me on my phone
My mum likes to moan
Because I'm always on my phone
I have an artistic mind
When it comes to art
Ask me to draw and I'll make the best.

Millie Corr (10)
St Helen's Primary School, Bishopbriggs

![YoungWriters Est. 1991]

This Is Oscar

Child genius
Writing makes me delirious
Most people don't take me serious
PE is my superpower
Maths is helping me every hour
Playing football I'll be battling for ball power
I can be sour or sweet
I love spice and heat
A rock in defence, I'll never be beat
My EAFC career mode is very neat.

Oscar Forde (11)
St Helen's Primary School, Bishopbriggs

Favourites Poem

T urtles are my favourite animals
H eights are my favourite
I love ice cream
S paghetti is my favourite

I love art, science, drawing and painting
S chool is so fun

M aths is the worst subject ever
E lephants are my mum's favourite animals.

Aailah Choudry (8)

St Helen's Primary School, Bishopbriggs

This Is Cian

I'm as pale as a ghost
Liked by most
As strange as a mage
I go to Spain to get rid of my pain
Blueish grey eyes
Just like the skies
Sometimes green like the trees
I'm white with a bite
I'm mystic and autistic
I don't give up easily
And I'm nice when I wanna be.

Cian Owens (11)
St Helen's Primary School, Bishopbriggs

Being Bradley

B ig brother Bradley, that's me
R eally great friend, everyone can see
A lways playing games
D rawing comic books is very fun
L ove my family, especially my mum
E veryone says I'm a kind boy
Y ou now know about Bradley.

Bradley McAllister (11)
St Helen's Primary School, Bishopbriggs

Winning

Rehaan is my name
That's all I wanna say
But I wanna be a pilot
But I better stay quiet
But KFC is all I want
Since food is my number one
And I like family
And swimming
Because in life
It's all about winning!

Mohammed Rehaan Choudry (11)

St Helen's Primary School, Bishopbriggs

This Is Me

G reat at gaming

A nd having loads of fun

M y big brother is super annoying but I love him loads

I magination booms from my head

N ot going to lie, I'm very competitive

G ood at football.

Finlay Lundie (11)

St Helen's Primary School, Bishopbriggs

This Is Me

A lyssa is my name

L ove to play football and PE too

Y ou really need to know I'm a middle child

S coring goals for my football team

S ister to Mia and Luca

A nd that's all about me.

Alyssa Graham (11)

St Helen's Primary School, Bishopbriggs

This Is Me!

Christopher is my name
Fantastic footwork is my game
Tell me to play defence and I will rock every game
You need a player, I am a catch
My keeper made a catch
He saved it without fail
I score again, c'mon The Vale.

Christopher McKechnie (10)
St Helen's Primary School, Bishopbriggs

This Is Me

A melia is my name
M y wee brother has a lot of fame
E lmer the elephant has a lot of shade
L ions live in a cage
I gloos are made in the winter
A rgh! I got a splinter.

Amelia Hampsey (11)

St Helen's Primary School, Bishopbriggs

This Is Me

Anton is my name
Skilful soccer is my game
Rocking Rossvale every match
My keeper always makes the catch
He punts it up without a fail
I score again,
C'mon The Vale!

Anthony Cosgrove (11)
St Helen's Primary School, Bishopbriggs

This Is Me

I'm as sweet as sugar
Don't worry, I don't bite.
I can make the sky blue
So that it is nice and bright.

If you're cold and lonely
I'll come to you right away
I can cheer you up
On a dull and rainy day.

On a lovely sunny day
I can be so funny
I'll make you laugh so hard
That your nose will go runny.

I'm helpful and I'm kind
Don't worry, I'll never commit a crime.

My least favourite subject is maths
Please don't ask any questions
It makes me go mad.

I had a dream about a fox in a hat
With a cat and a bag full of snacks

It had a big pile and I laughed for a while.

Kashana Mapemba (9)
St Joseph & St Teresa's Catholic Primary School, Woodlands

This Is Me

Ingredients:
A cup of happiness.
1 sprinkle of kindness.
A jug of talent.
A jug of funnyness.
1 sprinkle of bravery.
A teaspoon of strength.
A cup of learning.
A sprinkle of history.
A teaspoon of winter.
A cup of writing.

Now you need to mix it
First, you need to add a cup of happiness,
1 sprinkle of kindness and a teaspoon of talent
Put it into a bowl to stir.
Next, add 1 sprinkle of funniness,
1 sprinkle of bravery, a teaspoon of strength and a
cup of learning.
Bake for 20 minutes and top with 1 sprinkle of
history,
A teaspoon of winter and a cup of writing.

Now you have made me.
This is me.

Jacob Hodgson (10)

St Joseph & St Teresa's Catholic Primary School, Woodlands

All About Me

To make me you will need...
Believer powder.
A dash of happiness.
A bag of chicken nuggets.
A cute room.
A sprinkle of fun and mischief.
Also some sunglasses.

Firstly, get a bowl and then turn the oven to 100%.
Then add a dash of happiness.
Don't forget the believer powder.
After that add a bag of chicken nuggets and slowly add a cute bedroom.
Finally, sprinkle the fun and mischief
Then leave it to cool down then add the sunglasses.
This is me!

Sapphire-Rose Spencer (9)

St Joseph & St Teresa's Catholic Primary School, Woodlands

This Is Me

Ingredients to make me:
A sprinkle of kindness,
Half of a biscuit lover,
A dash of paint,
Half of a carrot,
A cupcake,
Lots of sprinkles,
A pinch of happiness,
A bar of chocolate,
Some ice cream,
A marshmallow.

Method:
Mix all together
Bake in the oven for 15 minutes
Add more sprinkles and icing
Add a pinch more of happiness
And lots of sugar
Then you have... Annalee!

Annalee Biggings (9)
St Joseph & St Teresa's Catholic Primary School, Woodlands

This Is Me

My dog, Nala, is the silliest dog.
She is the love of my life.
She is the one that I would take a bullet for
Or maybe even a knife.
I love her and she loves me as well.
I am her favourite, I can tell
My other dog is called Jed
They like to sleep at the end of my bed
They are the best dogs I could ever ask for.
In my family's eyes to their heart which is true
I love everyone
This is me.

Jethro Scott (8)

St Joseph & St Teresa's Catholic Primary School, Woodlands

This Is The Best Me

Football is my talent, I play with passion.
A goalkeeper at their best always needs a rest.
My passion for art is as big as my heart.
I was born very small, the smallest of all.
My dad calls me Trigger but I'm also a good singer.
I was born on the 9th of November and my name is Summer.
I have a big appetite, I also love a good pillow fight.
Sleeping and fishing are the best.

Summer Nelson (10)

St Joseph & St Teresa's Catholic Primary School, Woodlands

This Is Me

I am a...
Chocolate chomper,
Biscuit monster,
Ice cream lover,
Sweetie stealer,
Popcorn cruncher,

This is me

Football player,
Funny worm,
Silly billy,
Excited hopper,
Always playful,
Sometimes funny,
Silly sausage

This is me

I am a...
Animal lover,
Spider hater,

Pet owner,
Game player,

This is me.

Ellie Wrafter-Saxton (8)

St Joseph & St Teresa's Catholic Primary School, Woodlands

This Is Me

I am a lovely girl
I am a strong person
I am a very chatty girl
I am a tidy person
I am a sporty girl
I am a happy person
I'm as silly as a frog
I am silly
I am a pizza lover
I am a mash hater
I am a chocolate lover
I am an ice cream lover
I am a holiday lover
I am a pool lover
I am a Spain lover
This is me.

Skyla Wilkinson (8)

St Joseph & St Teresa's Catholic Primary School, Woodlands

This Is Me

Ice cream gobbler,
Biscuit robber,
Chocolate eater,
Crispy sneaker,
Takeaway getaway,
This is me!

Liver deliverer,
Stealer dealer,
Furious curious,
Frightened brightened,
Good boy, bad girl,
Good girl, bad boy,
Football, basketball,
Baseball, volleyball.

This is *me!*

Maxim Pavlovskij (8)

St Joseph & St Teresa's Catholic Primary School, Woodlands

This Is Me

I have brown eyes
I have brown hair
I like gymnastics
I like baking
I like swimming
I like pepperoni pizza
I like fizzy pop
I like energy drinks
I like dogs
I like chocolate
I like Christmas
I like Halloween
I like going abroad
This is me.

Sapphire Wright (10)
St Joseph & St Teresa's Catholic Primary School, Woodlands

All About Me

I like baking cakes
And swimming in lakes.
I love eating pasta
And drinking faster.
I like chilling
And treadmilling.
I love dancing
And glancing.
I like singing
And blinging.
I like watching a series
That has good theories.

This is me!

Libby Headrigi (10)

St Joseph & St Teresa's Catholic Primary School, Woodlands

This Is Me!

I am a...
Awesome helper
Chicken and pig lover
Noise maker
Book reader
Bird watcher
Cricket player
Horse rider
And last but not least...
Conker fighter.

Flynn O'Connell (7)
St Joseph & St Teresa's Catholic Primary School, Woodlands

The Amazing Kamran

A dog lover

M akes cakes

A m nice to people who are nice

Z ebras are cool

I am sad all the time

N ot annoying

G ets excited when it's Christmas.

Kamran Buck (9)

St Margaret's CE Primary School, Horsforth

Swimming Is My Favourite

I was chilling in a pool,
Where it was madly hot and cool,
Nice and sunny,
I got out of the pool,
And had chocolate,
I sat down to eat.

Jenson Stewart (9)
St Margaret's CE Primary School, Horsforth

All About Me

I am Adrijus, a Year 5,
I enjoy watching YouTube when they are live.
A boy with obnoxious hair,
When I am near my brother, we have an affair.
In my life, I've met some pretty nice blokes,
But I also get angry when my mother smokes.
Sometimes when I wake up for school,
I think *argh, not cool!*
My favourite fast food restaurant is Burger King,
But I lose it when I drop my onion ring.
My favourite subject is maths,
Just as I enjoy my bubble baths.
I have a cat called Roxy,
When she doesn't get what she wants she acts
quite foxy.
I hope you have learned something new about me,
As this poem is all about me.

Adrijus Zygmantas (9)
St Mary's CE Primary School, Hinckley

All About Me

This is me,
A passion for fashion,
A perfect fit,
I love to add and subtract.
It's my thing to be with my friend,
They're precious like a blinding gem.
Indoors some days to make a sweet treat and share.
I always have a pencil in my hand for the ideas in my heart.
I love to sing 'It's a New World',
When a song drops a beat I'm out of my seat,
I'm an artistic freak,
I love to draw and show ideas,
It's something I was born with.
I love snow, it snowed the day I was born,
I'm never cold,
I love the stars 'cause I'm a shooting star.
I love the dead of night, it's beautiful like a glittery gem.
I love my athletic and smart personality,

It's a thing that won't leave my heart
Like the love for my parents and pets
Especially my adorable fluffy grey kitten.

Amelia Davies (9)

St Mary's CE Primary School, Hinckley

All About Me

At home I stay and say hooray,
With my dog, I play.
Charlie likes to tug and hug.
When I put him in his crate,
He starts to hate.
When I give him a treat,
He starts to eat.

I love to eat Italian food,
It puts me in a good mood.
I like to drink tea,
It makes me happy!
I like to eat meat
And it's like a treat.

I made it to Area Sports
And I lost to the final four.
Maybe I will run as fast as the speed of light,
Hopefully one day.

Isaac Linton (10)
St Mary's CE Primary School, Hinckley

This Is Me

I'm sitting in my bed, colouring in red.

I'm funny at times and I also like to rhyme.

I love swimming with my friends and I can do a back bend.

I have two cats and my sister has two rats.

I read diary-type books and I like feeding the ducks.

I'm not pale but I like false nails.

I wear glasses but I have nice long lashes.

This is me, Lucia.

Lucia Harrison (11)
St Mary's CE Primary School, Hinckley

This Is Me

T rying to go swimming
H ave time to read Harry Potter
I have four cats and five kittens
S hort in height

I have three friends
S leep is good for me

M ake cakes with my sisters
E very type of pizza to enjoy.

This is me, Morgan.

Morgan Stevens (11)
St Mary's CE Primary School, Hinckley

This Is Me!

I am a...
Singer and music is my thing
I feel good when I start to sing
I can never stop
Dancing when I hear the beat
Floating around my heart like a dazzling fleet
Music keeps me going when I'm down and sad.

Ethan Oppong (9)
St Mary's CE Primary School, Hinckley

All About Me

I'm from Poland
But I live in England.
After school,
I eat food
And I'm always in a good mood.
I ride on my bike
And I play with my friends,
That's all I do
But I'm also a laugher.

Kamil Czarnecki (11)
St Mary's CE Primary School, Hinckley

A Baby

When giving food it's a mess,
When you pull a funny face it giggles and smiles,
If it cries go and give it a hug,
When hungry give it some milk,
When tired put her down in bed,
If bored give her a toy.

Harry Proctor (11)
St Mary's CE Primary School, Hinckley

ADHD

It is quite hard to listen
Also, to stop talking when I've been told
Sometimes I get told off because I can't stop laughing!
I can get very angry and I can't control myself
So I hit people!
Also, some people say to me, "Calm down," and I say I can't.

Isaac Waterman (10)

St Mary's Church Of England
(Voluntary Aided) Primary School, Swanley

This Is Me - Toby

Toby is my name
Football is in my blood
My mum is a hero
My cat is a cutie
Manchester is my team
Fortnite is my game
Riding bikes is great fun
My eyes are blue like marbles
I hate onions, but I love tomatoes
Kickboxing is my favourite sport!

This is me.

Andis (Toby) Kalnins (11)
St Patrick's Primary School, Moneymore

My Life - Rap

I am rapping these bars
One day I want to go to Mars.
Or become a boxer
Punch holes through cars.
Or become an accountant
And get some green money
The way that I rap, don't you think I am funny?
I want to drive a rose-red Ferrari
In the screeching hot sun.
Or become a gorilla
But hurt no one.
I want to fly a kite over the crystal-blue sea.
If you're sad, you can count on me.
But if I am angry, leave me be.
Everyone is different.
I am me.

Sidney Jubb (9)
St Robert Southwell Catholic Primary School, Horsham

This Is Me

I felt worried when I first started school.

I feel anxious when I'm alone.

I feel frustrated when I get the answer incorrect.

I worried when I first started school.

I felt nervous when I entered Year 5.

I feel furious when people make fun of me.

I feel provoked when I get woken up.

I feel embarrassed when my friends tell a secret about me.

I feel joyful when I play with my friends.

I feel loved when I get a hug from my mum.

I feel proud when I score a try for my team.

Santiago Fernandes (9)

St Robert Southwell Catholic Primary School, Horsham

This Is Me

I am a
Book reader
Honey craver
Lego player
Army man creator
Rugby tackler

Historical expert
Chocolate chomper
Early riser
Horror hater
Loathsome hiker.

Theo Strutt (9)

St Robert Southwell Catholic Primary School, Horsham

This Is Me

Sibling smasher
Skill crusher
Neck cracker
Spider lover
Shark wanter
Black Hawk downer
Football fan.

Ronnie Digweed Ball (10)

St Robert Southwell Catholic Primary School, Horsham

Myself

First, gather happiness and fun
Stir in big parties and adventure
Season with energy and delicious chocolate
Add a pinch of bananas and chocolate sauce
Pour in some sprinkles and a bucket of loyalty
Add a cup of dreams with chocolate bananas
Blend tickles, joy and personality
Then warm gently with a bunny.

Labaika Mahmood (9)
St Thomas CE Primary School, Werneth

The Sporty Me

T ough when I have a problem.

H elpful at carrying heavy things.

E xploring king when it comes to fun places.

S porty kid and of course I am strong.

P uffy hair when it comes to head injuries.

O f course I am sporty.

R unning kid when races are involved.

T all when it comes to height-restricted things.

Y es, I am powerful.

M uch faster than you think.

E xercising is my speciality.

This is the sporty me.

Saleh Altaf (9)
Welton Primary School, Brough

Football

F riends

O vercoming your fear

O utstanding

T eam

B alanced

A thletic

L oyal

L ife.

Annabel Jones (10)

Whirley Primary School, Macclesfield

My Family

F riends

A pples

M ummy

I ndividual

L ittle sister

Y ell.

Bella Hill (10)

Whirley Primary School, Macclesfield

This Is Me

My name is Tilly
My brother thinks I'm silly
I like to walk my dogs by the sea
My favourite drink is probably tea
My hair is my best feature
And I think cows are the best creature
I often make a mess and I don't like cress
I like Christmas because it's merry
My favourite fruit is a strawberry
I'm as wise as an owl
And I think the smell of pumpkin is foul
I like music with a bang and sweets with a tang
I hate slowly walking but I really like talking
I'm like a tree dancing in the sun
My favourite meal is burgers and buns.

Matilda King (11)
Windlesham School & Nursery, Brighton

This Is Me!

A mazing

N ice

D arts is fun

R unning keeps you fit

E ating healthy food

W onderful.

Andrew Sloss-Hartley (8)

Woodlawn Primary School, Carrickfergus

This Is Me

A haiku

I am a gamer
Gaming with my wee brother
I love Liverpool

This is me.

Riley O'Lynn (8)
Woodlawn Primary School, Carrickfergus

This Is Me

A haiku

I love Liverpool.
Favourite team is the Springboks,
Libbok is the best.

Freddie Anderson (9)
Woodlawn Primary School, Carrickfergus

This Is Me!

K ind

O riginal

B est

I ntelligent.

Kobi Wylie (9)

Woodlawn Primary School, Carrickfergus

This Is Me

A haiku

Trampoline is fun
Love to play with my sister
Gaming is so fun!

Zac Berry (8)

Woodlawn Primary School, Carrickfergus

This Is Me

A haiku

I enjoy hockey
It makes me very happy.
And I like to swim.

Ellie Whiteside (8)

Woodlawn Primary School, Carrickfergus

This Is Me

A haiku

I like to play games,
I go to the caravan,
I support Linfield.

Noah Hollis (8)

Woodlawn Primary School, Carrickfergus

Young Writers Est. 1991

YOUNG WRITERS INFORMATION

We hope you have enjoyed reading this book – and that you will continue to in the coming years.

If you're the parent or family member of an enthusiastic poet or story writer, do visit our website **www.youngwriters.co.uk/subscribe** and sign up to receive news, competitions, writing challenges and tips, activities and much, much more! There's lots to keep budding writers motivated!

If you would like to order further copies of this book, or any of our other titles, then please give us a call or order via your online account.

Young Writers
Remus House
Coltsfoot Drive
Peterborough
PE2 9BF
(01733) 890066
info@youngwriters.co.uk

Join in the conversation!
Tips, news, giveaways and much more!

f YoungWritersUK 🐦 YoungWritersCW 📷 youngwriterscw

Scan me to watch the
This Is Me video!